NAME

DATES

STEWART, TABORI & CHANG

NEW YORK

INTRODUCTION

I have been creating paintings and silkscreens with patriotic themes for many years. It is only since the Blue Dog series, which I began some fifteen years ago, that I have felt more like an American artist than a regional, Cajun artist. I am proud to be from the United States of America. It is our spirit—strong in the symbol of our flag—which has always been a testimony of our strength, courage, and compassion.

When you set out to create something new, to give voice or expression to the inner working of your imagination, you are embarking on a journey of self-discovery. Once your creation—be it a painting, a sketch, or simply a few written reflections—is complete, it can teach you a little something about yourself. There's no doubt that the Blue Dog series continues to do that for me.

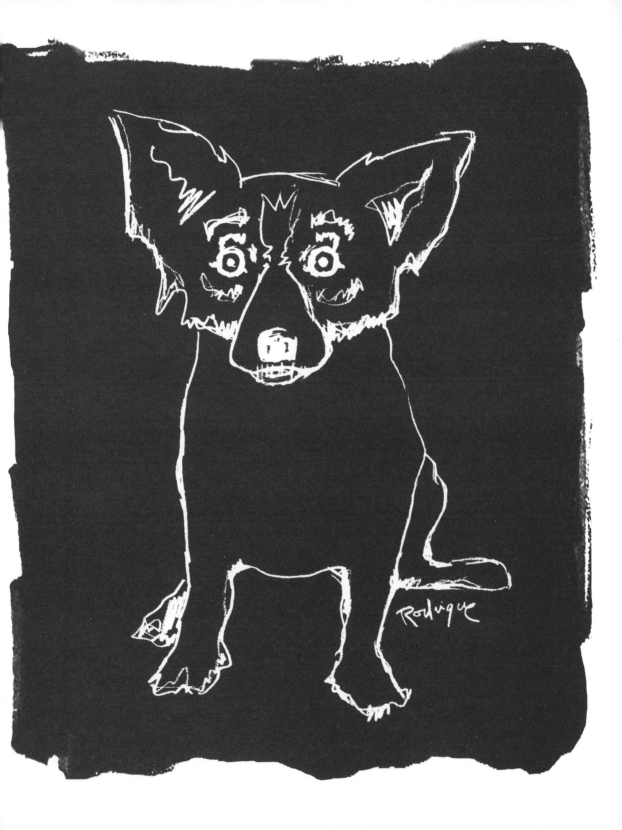

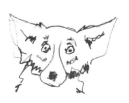

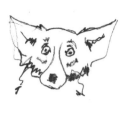

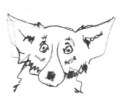

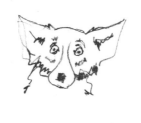

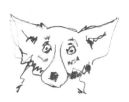

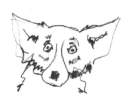

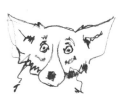

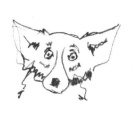

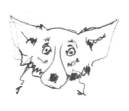

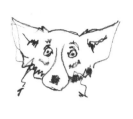

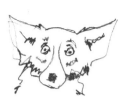

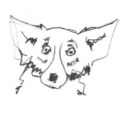

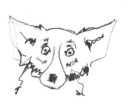

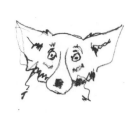

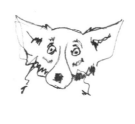

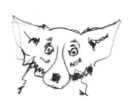

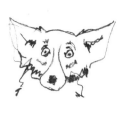

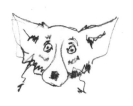

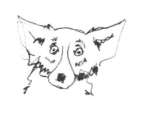

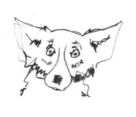

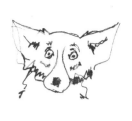

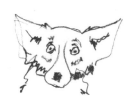

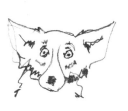

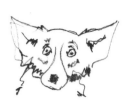

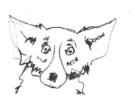

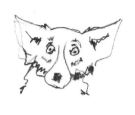

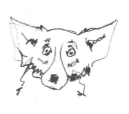

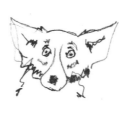

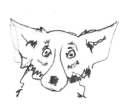

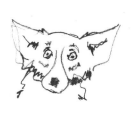

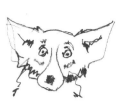

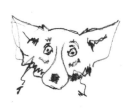

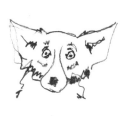

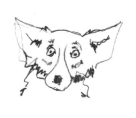

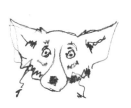

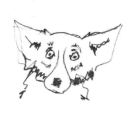

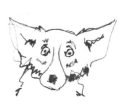

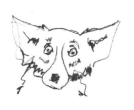

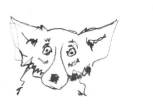

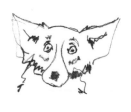

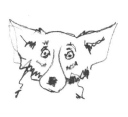

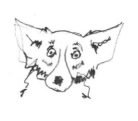

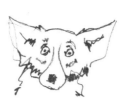

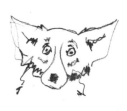

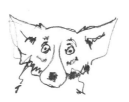

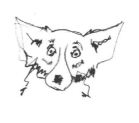

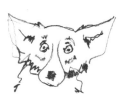

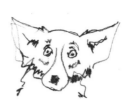

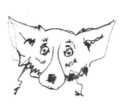

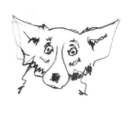

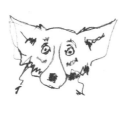

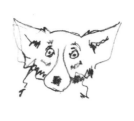

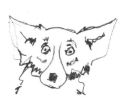

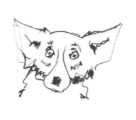

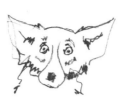

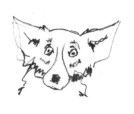

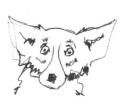

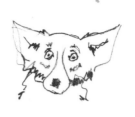

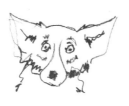

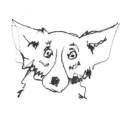

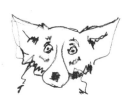

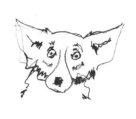

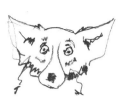

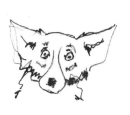

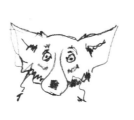

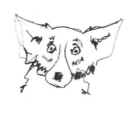

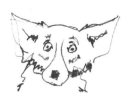

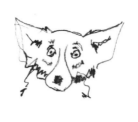

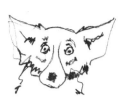

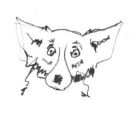

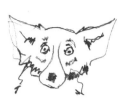

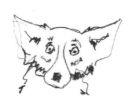

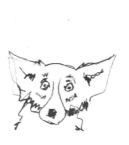

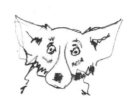

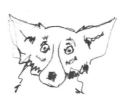

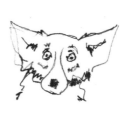

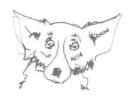

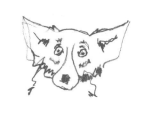

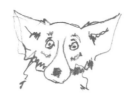

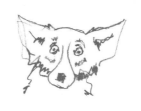

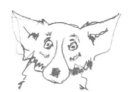

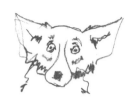

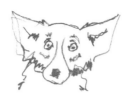

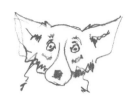

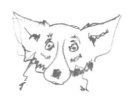

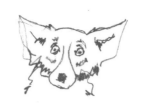

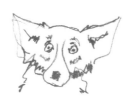

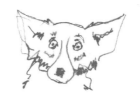

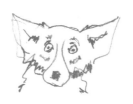

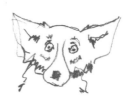

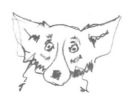

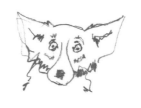

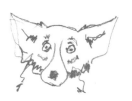

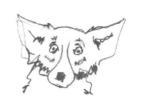

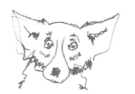

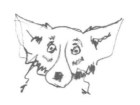

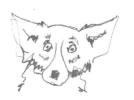

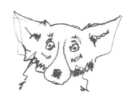

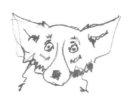

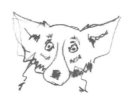

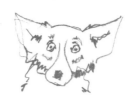

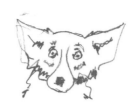

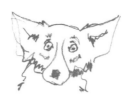

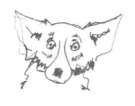

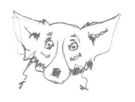

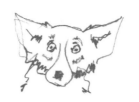

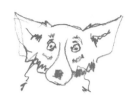

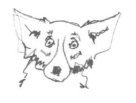

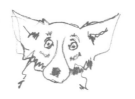

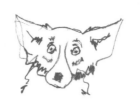

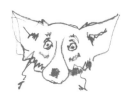

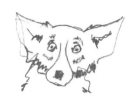

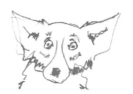

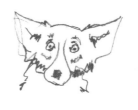

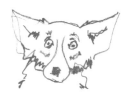

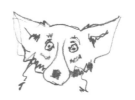

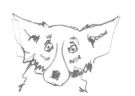

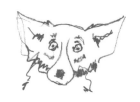

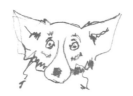

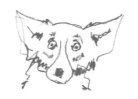

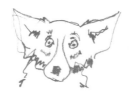

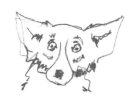

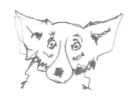

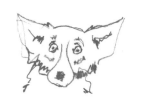

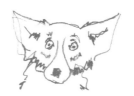

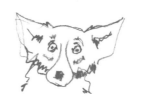

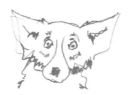

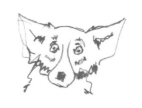

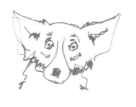

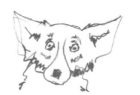

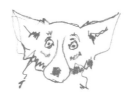

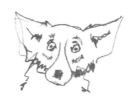

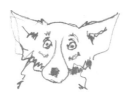

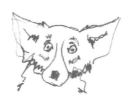

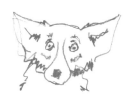

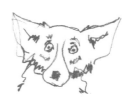

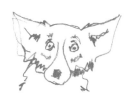

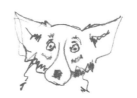

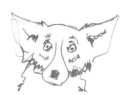

Project editor: Sandra Gilbert
Production: Kim Tyner

Published in 2001 by
Stewart, Tabori & Chang
A Company of La Martinière Groupe
115 West 18th Street
New York, NY 10011

Export Sales to all countries except Canada,
France, and French-speaking Switzerland:
Thames and Hudson Ltd.
181A High Holborn
London WC1V 7QX
England

Canadian Distribution:
Canadian Manda Group
One Atlantic Avenue, Suite 105
Toronto, Ontario M6K 3E7
Canada

ISBN: 1-58479-213-2

Printed in China
1 3 5 7 9 10 8 6 4 2
First Printing